white lipstick

white lipstick

poems

GERI DIGIORNO

Red Hen Press Los Angeles

White Lipstick

Cover art: Yvonne Baynes

Book design by Michael Vukadinovich
Cover Design by Mark E. Cull

ISBN: 1-59709-017-4
Library of Congress Catalog Card Number: 2004118151

Published by Red Hen Press

The City of Los Angeles Cultural Affairs Department, California Arts Council, Los Angeles County Arts Commission and National Endowment for the Arts partially support Red Hen Press.

First Edition

acknowledgments

Some of these poems have previously appeared in *33 Review,* *Bogg, Carbuncle, Cyanosis, Fishtrap, The Haight Ashbury Literary Journal, Paterson Literary Review, Sonoma Mandala, tight, The Tomcat*, and *Women's Voices* and were collected in *I'm Tap Dancing*, a chapbook by Norton Coker Press.

To Tony who changed my life and showed me how to be real, to Michelle who showed me how to survive, to Yvonne and Rick for their constant love and support, and to Judy who thought of the title for this book and always stayed my best friend.

I'd also like to thank Al Young who showed me it was ok to write the truth, Diane di Prima, a wondrous teacher and friend, MZ. D. who inspires by divine influence, Maria Mazziotti Gillan who inspires me to write every time I hear her read. John Mendel who sang Elvis songs to me over the phone and Stephanie Mendel who encouraged me to get this book together, Rich Benbrook, Joseph Millar, Katy Dang, my writing group: Gail, Lynn, Godelieve and Judy, Trendy Studios with Diane Di Prima and Nell Melcher, and my first writing teacher, Rene Chavez.

Thanks also to John and Karla, Rick and Sue, Yvonne and Henry, the extraordinary Mifflin sisters and to my grandchildren: Nichole, Jessica, John, Richard, Tanya, Anthony, Wendy, Julie, and great-grandson Drake.

contents

white lipstick

i o u

aunt yvonne
was marcelling my hair
she gave me a quarter
to keep still
i put it in my mouth
i don't know why
god knows there's nothing tasty
about metal
i was sitting there
clicking the silver
against my teeth
turning it over and
over with my tongue
as auntie
parted and curved
her way down the
side of my head
somehow i swallowed
the thing
only it got stuck
half way down my throat
i started choking
and turning blue
aunt yvonne reached
right down there
with her long nails
and lifted it out
i named my first child
after her
actually
i think it was
a buffalo nickel

red jello

i can see right through
to the flowered plate
from my mother's house
sitting on the black and white
oil cloth like a circle
on a tic tac toe square

next door mr rivera's roses
climb the fence to the two by four
nailed there for the clothes line
flying kite tail colors in the afternoon

rocky the boxer dog walks back
and forth on the cement patio
like james cagney pacing
the prison yard where mother sits
a heating pad and pillows
the newspaper folded
to the crossword puzzle
and a pencil

between the rooftops
a points down
wedge of bay
opaque whiteness
against a cloud washed sky

on mona's side a mirror
her makeup sits
like some strange spaceship
landed in the land of oz
flashing iridescent ovals

on the mustard walls
her cigarette smoke
coming straight up
from the ashtray
in a thin blue line

kickball and tampons

i am waiting
waiting for something
to happen

all the time playing
kickball with the boys
outside my house

a nervousness
a quaking
a time of change

playing hide and seek
or roller skating with my sisters
in a wide circle as wide as
the black street

floating here above everything
deep inside me
the ocean washing against the shore

aunt ada

i was named after my aunt ada
a trick-rider in the rodeo
in utah
when my father took us back
to stay with her for a year
she didn't ride anymore
allergic she said
she cooked on a coal stove
that heated the small iron
she pressed our clothes with

when we bathed
she started with the largest child
adding hot water with each new addition
until a bunch of us smaller kids
ended up in a pee-warm puddle
she made the best milk gravy
i've ever tasted from skimmed milk
in winter uncle barkley
took us ice-skating on the frozen pond
attaching ice skates to our shoes

that christmas
the tree was without lights
decorated with homemade trim
it didn't snow until january
when it did snow
we kids sat stapled to the bedroom window
watching uncle chop the heads off chickens
their headless forms jumping and cavorting
like baseball players
spewing red tobacco juice on a field of white

that night we sat bug-eyed
as a large platter of fried chicken
was passed around the table
my sister and i excused ourselves
and sat staring
at the dark corner of the yard
where the rabbit hutch stood

balls

in junior high
my friends and i
had a club called
"balls"
we stood around at
lunch time singing
"balls balls we are balls
sour-balls lemon-balls sugar-balls butter-balls"
that's when the dean of girls
called us into her office
told us it was against the law
to have a club
made us promise to break it up
that's when we went underground
with secret signals
double and triple dutch
meetings before school
at the a-1 bakery on 24th street
where we'd all gather and eat
jelly donuts
until that christmas
when joanie and i
were sitting on my front steps
singing jingle balls
and my older sister
went into the house
and told my father

at sutro baths

that summer they held us
on their shoulders in the pool
the hardness of their heads
between our legs
our long wet limbs hanging down
their chests
their hands
holding onto our ankles
like handcuffs
each team trying to upset the other

after
we lay on wet towels
at the side of the pool
on cold cement
the boys hung over us
on their elbows
trying to talk us into
whatever they could

pleading with us
just to let them feel us
"i won't do anything
i promise"

as if we held their future
in our bodies
as if they couldn't go on
with their lives
unless we let them
as if they would be in pain
for days

what about us?

helen sanchez was born without big toes

we played underneath
her dining room table
ate brown squares of
ice cream her mother

served us from a tray
jesus nailed to a cross
hung from her wall
his sad eyes rolled up

toward the ceiling
and then i saw mary
holding baby jesus her
mournful face already

knowing what his fate
would be her plump heart
wrapped in thorns and
white roses a sword stuck

through the middle
fire leaping out the top
and helen saying jesus
died for all our sins

and me reaching for
my toes

i'm one of them

i was baptized at sixteen
in my sister mona's white
two piece bathing suit
and white flannel night gown

laid back onto the water by two men
in alabaster suits
holding my nose
while they prayed over me
pushed me down underneath the coolness
till i came up saved

legs

in the bathroom at alvarado school
girls stood on their hands
tipped their bodies up
in the air and paused
before their tennis shoes found the wall
their skirts hiding their faces
underpants pleated and puckered
between their legs

sometimes there were crude falls
a sideways crash scraped knees
but mostly it was the guts and gusto of it all
not smooth you have to understand
these were brave girls not acrobats
not trim or necessarily fit
just school girls tumbling against gray walls

giggling girls and smart talk
pushing and peeing girls
throwing their bodies
over and over
one by one

i did it with them
in my mind

i found that wall

the little woman

mother was a little under five feet
bought her shoes in the children's department
wore tiny hats with veils and bows
baked canned cooked and gardened
and sewed all our clothes
carefully positioning the pattern pieces
to get the most out of each bolt of cloth

when world war two came
ethel mae went to work in the ship yards
wore overalls and a cap
tilted to one side
on blond bobbed curls
she was given an award
for showing them
how to get more parts
cut from each piece
of sheet metal

kools

at fourteen my girlfriends and i sat
in roosevelt's tamale parlor on 24th street
and practiced french inhaling
curling smoke up our noses bette davis style
we ordered cheese enchiladas with rice
in mole sauce and tall frosty bottles of coca-cola
the boys practiced smoke rings blowing
dreamlike circles in the air (like the
smoke signals in an old roy rogers movie)
the trick was to put your finger through
the center before the lariats and lassos
disappeared forever

it could have been summer

july
it was a black lamb
i remember
and my sisters
setting me on the porch
to see it tethered
on a rope out back
it was white they said
the heat burning at my elbows
my neck
the wooden porch bleached
pure and my sisters
disappearing in tall grass
flowers blooming on their dresses
parasols shading their eyes
that night wild dogs
tore at its throat
white lamb
soaked black with blood

mona

there were things she loved
beside herself

putting things on layaway
hanging out at bars
nursing one drink all night

she fell in love with tom
who liked to look at his reflection
in the mirror at the cork n bottle

he left her when she lost the baby
it broke her heart

there were things she loved beside herself
off color jokes she retold
often leaving out the punch line
she worked as an usherette
at the golden gate on market street

there were things she loved beside herself
enameled boxes good purses and shoes
costume jewelry being engaged
she tried it five or six times

there were things she loved beside herself
designer clothes
she bought at upscale resale shops in the city
egg yolk facials
the red compact that left a perfect circle
in the window on diamond street

she had her breakdown at the bluebird café
on mother's birthday
it rained the night they took her to
san francisco general

my mother sewing

the gate leg table in the dining room
padded and covered with blankets and sheets
so that the whole surface could be used
for pinning and cutting and pressing
each pattern piece

my mother's small hands like a child's
so precise everything so exact
each pattern piece
angled and positioned to save material
the smell of fingers and fabric
the iron steaming scissors sharp and ready
my mother humming under her breath

this is when my mother fitted me
pins sticking out of her mouth
me standing in my slip
her fingers cool next to my skin
fitting the fabric pieces
on my small body

the way she handled the cloth
like it was alive
me
standing still standing still

when people ask me
did your mother hold you?
this is what I remember

on dolores street

some nights i babysat
for my sister
who lived in a flat
with her two children
her husband across the bay
in san quentin

feeding the kids canned spaghetti
and fishsticks
for dessert we wet our fingers
and dipped them into kool-aid crystals
the tart taste staining our tongues
at night curled wallpaper strips

hung down the hall to the
front door
and I slept in what seemed
like a bottom bunk

in a dark and dusty room
and listened to my sister
and her sailor boyfriend
grapple in the next room

the old couch moaned and creaked
like a ship at sea

freewheeling

when billy powell
totaled his bike
running into some lady's car
she gave him a new one
my father
picked up the broken pieces
took some plumbing pipe
and welded me a silver bike

it took me a week
of hanging onto the
pink stucco next door
before i got my balance
once i took off
i was free

flying up and down the block
racing with the boys on diamond hill
coasting down twenty-fourth street
pumping up hills
breaking down castro
riding with the wind

the e names

they came in souped-up hot rods
chopped down versions
of some future car
chrome motor mounts
low window frames glistening
in neon lights reflecting
young girls in skirts
tight to the ankles
scuffed white duck shoes
and rolled down socks
angora sweaters
buttoned down the back
white lipstick bright scarves
tied around their necks

the boys in dirty down levis
that stood in the corner
by themselves white t-shirts
a short pack of camels
rolled up in the sleeve
their hair combed into
a perfect d.a.
an i.d. bracelet
on a silver chain
boys with spit polished
double soled shoes
with taps on the heels

they congregated
at the drive-in restaurants
car hops dressed in dance shorts
and roller skates cropped jackets
and smart caps angled
on flushed faces
balanced trays filled
with strawberry shakes
sizzling fries covered with salt
hot juicy hamburgers
with sliced tomatoes red onions
and a pickle

with names like betty
shirley margie and judy
The e names

so what's the worst that could happen?

upstairs blackout curtains
hung from our windows
sometimes
on moonless nights
we'd hide under our pillows
listening for planes
as sirens wailed
or peer into
the black on black
looking for some image
seeing the phantom whiteness
of the air-raid captain's hat

in the daylight
we studied aircraft
so we'd know our own
and bought war stamps at school

the red pocket knife

i remember my father
cutting into the white
flesh of an apple
the red skin spiraling down
like new years streamers
he did the same with oranges
the thick rind winding upward
toward the glint of steel
you could take the empty peel
in your cupped hands
and reform it
back to its original shape
he did the same with pencils
trimming the soft wood
into perfect points
with perfect scalloped edges
and one time i remember
when our car broke down
somewhere between reno and sacramento
the night dead black like coal
and daddy whittling a wooden plug
for the engine
we kids sat at bare tables
in an empty cafe watching my father
shivering in the pale glow
of a single electric bulb
casting an eerie spell
on him and the men helping
their voices floating
in the dark half-light
voices soft like the lighted wood
flying around my fathers fingers

stuffed peppers

my mother was gone
living up in oregon
with ralph mckenna
at fourteen
i was the oldest
still living at home

my father gave me
money for food
i went to my sister
to ask what to cook

back home
i boiled rice
par-boiled peppers
browned ground beef
added tomato sauce
baked it in the oven
for one hour

that night
my father smiled and ate
and asked for more
later he told me
he never did like
stuffed peppers

for breakfast
we ate my father's
oatmeal mush
flecked with raisins
and burnt black scrapings
and waited
for my mother
to come home again

he always took her back

at the national cemetery
in san bruno i search a sea
of bleached dominos on green felt
counting trees from the road
looking for familiar names

they put my father down deeper
to make room for my mother
they share the same marker

mother had moved back home
after her second husband died
when father became ill
my parents went to redwood city
to remarry so mother would be
taken care of

each time i go i take
a little of them home with me
to scrape off into my flower bed
i think they like that

i grew up in noe valley

i grew up in noe valley
in san francisco and fell in love
with the newspaper boy
on 24th and castro

as a man i would be different
i could ask ladies out
fuck them and leave them
i would be boss and
i would be just as chickenshit
as i am now

in the blue house
the rooms are small
the garden green
with grass and grass and flowers

all night long
i danced my head off
every man wanted me
i stood them all off
it worked and now
i was alone but
i didn't mind at all

all the moonlight and
the cool cool breeze
come in come in
the apple tree is tall
i cut the top off
three years ago

i swam a long time
my arms coming up in arches
i pulled myself out
dripping onto the hot sidewalk
gray circles hitting the cement

i fell in love with a boy
who stood on the corner
of 24th and castro
selling newspapers
he was young so was i
12 or 13
good brown hair
that lay on his head
in soft waves
his shoes were scuffed
tan cords worn at the knees
he stood in front of cleggs drug store
one foot of papers stacked
on stacked on stacked

when i look in the mirror
i see my father
i have his eyes
high forehead
i am tall like him
with wide shoulders
we walk the same way
the veins in my hands stand out
just like his he was
a soft and thoughtful man

the street cars come by
every fifteen minutes
i fell in love with a boy
who stood on the corner
in front of cleggs
tan cords thinned at the knees
good brown hair that matched his shoes
with one foot of stacked papers
against the building
a large rock holding them down
and cried out *newspaper,*
get your newspaper here

later when the stack was gone
we met at the show
he put his arm around
the back of my seat and
told me how much he loved
the way i chewed my gum

one year later

one year later
i will be living
in a home for
unwed mothers
in oakland

right there in black and white
i am fifteen years old
standing between
dorothy hardy and
joan luhring
jim cancella behind us
in a light suit and tie
a mouth full of teeth
like a cold breeze

joan is wearing a white
two-piece dress
with matching heels
her lips open
marilyn monroe style
albino curls oppose
her bony features
dorothy's dress
sweeps away behind her
outlining heavy legs
thick brown locks
cut short
surround her dimples

i'm the only one
not smiling
dark blondness falls
across my cheeks
my eyes tumble
to the ground
diploma tightly held
in both hands

wonder woman

straddling your 37 buick
and you
on hill street
above my house
humping each other
on the floor
on 24th street
over nagles deli
taking the twenty 22nd street steps
on my plumbers bike
standing up all the way down
chugging turpentine cocktails
on diamond street
trying to abort
trying to abort
ron's little sister tessie
killing herself
with a coat hanger

saving it

at booth memorial
home for unwed mothers
i joined the choir group
where we sang in flowing robes
that covered our protruding bellies

the salvation army ladies
preached to us about our sins
encouraged us to come on down
and get saved

i wouldn't go
i was the only girl
in their long history
who wouldn't give it up
for jesus

i had already given it up
in the back of a 37 buick

my first husband

i
saw
you
tooling
up
mission
street
in
a
red
convertible
covered
with
girls
little did i know
it would be you
who'd break
my
cherry
my
heart
my
life
my
back
my
spirit
my
self
my
my
my
my
my
my
my

my first poem

i was 21
stuck in daly city
with 3 kids
no car
and longfellow

the fog came in
the roof leaked
i transplanted weeds
caught a rat
sang in bed
waited
for my husband
to come home
and wrote this poem:

i'd like to die o my to die
but all I ever do is cry

it went on like that
for 20 or 30 lines
and
i
did
die

$37.50 a month

we inherited the place
from bill's mother
been in the family
since before ww ii
passed from one
family member
to another
the rent never changing

we moved
from a flat
on duncan and delores
a corner second story
with bay windows and cockroaches
where my oldest
yvonne then two
locked me on the roof
when i was hanging clothes

on 24th and noe i hung clothes
from the porch
on great lines
that stretched from the building
to a tall pole on the sidewalk
weighed down
with blankets and sheets
once the line gave way
and hung down the dirty wall
like a broken vow

i can see my daughters
like an old
black and white photograph
sitting on the back steps
in their party dresses

dark transparent
wings of bugs
hanging on their lips
waiting for their
young father
out playing with his friends
waiting for us
to grow up
and be their parents

every day he played the same tune

"i'm leaving on a jet plane
don't know when i'll be back again"

and then one day
he packed a few belongings
into a hat-box overnighter
i won at the monthly avon meeting
and headed up south city
to talk penny into leaving
her two small children and her husband
and moving in with him and she did

and here we all are
twenty years later
him and me and our three kids
and penny
taking pictures and trying on hats
at my house after breakfast
and he asks me why
did i cut off all my hair

marilyn and me

my husband thought she was sexy
i was 21 with 3 kids

at home he dressed me
in tight skirts
sweaters and high-heels
posed me on the wooden bench
in our kitchen
my legs stretched out in front of me
one knee higher than the other
my head resting against ivy wallpaper

he took photographs
carried copies in his wallet

i dreamed of marilyn
her sad sweet face
moving across the screen

in the movie *the misfits*
marilyn
playing roslyn taber
tells clark gable

maybe all there is
is the next thing that happens

love

i was in it
up to my ears

i could hear
music playing
in the background

it wasn't love really
just me
wanting to be
somebody

i fell into it
like a broken branch
carried down a rushing stream

to the open sea

when i left my house

on winding way in belmont
i took the old chevy convertible
with the shredded top
my four-poster bed
the jade plant in the clay pot
my books
bike
the boston rocker
and my blue dishes

i left the tie-dyed sheets
the green curtains i bought
when i was selling avon
the busted t-bird in the driveway
the contents of the kitchen table
spattered on the walls
the flying chair that caught him
right behind the knee as he
kept walking out the door
and my fake leopard skin coat
which he used to reupholster
the footstool from his
mother's house

stripping wallpaper

old patterns come into view
the daly city house
we bought with our refund check
and the cadillac you and fat john
primed and molded

we had to give the irs money back
to the bankruptcy court
remember they took my wedding rings too
i have no need for plaids or roses
now i want my walls stripped bare

listen last week i was discussing
poetry with my plumber frank
and i remembered you're not dead
but living in redding
i thought we must have had something
between us besides the kids

i mean i remember things you did

back then i would have painted over
all those layers
you wanted to unwrap that room
reveal its narrow windows
diffused light

we went through years and years of wallpaper

her last movie

a photograph
of marilyn monroe
leaning against
a wood plank wall
her face in shadow
she looks rested
her eyes and mouth closed
hands clasped together
over her stomach

she's wearing a dress
covered with cherries
with stems like
drifting balloons
a spear of light cuts across
her breasts
her hand a garish red
misshapen claw

you could turn the picture
sideways
and make it her coffin
her blond hair thick
like sculpted stone

shirley betty spider and rudy

for Todd Moore

shirley worked
in the cannery
in fresno her
big voice matched
her frame she wore
delicate scarves
and too much make-
up her boyfriend
spider was a bum
they lived in her
late brother's
house with his dog
named betty one
time at the play-
house bar spider
sold the dog for
fifteen dollars
to a man named
rudy and told
shirley it had
jumped overboard
while he was fish-
ing when she found
out she got the dog
back but refused
to pay the extra
twenty dollars rudy
paid to have it
groomed she should
have taken spider
fishing but she was
afraid she couldn't
find another man

mona was

in the ungraded class
at alvarado school
graduated from
james lick jr. high
got a job
as an usherette
at the golden gate
on market street
became a candy girl
at the esquire theatre
was engaged five

or six times
mother disapproved

mona had
one marriage
one dead baby
one divorce
one breakdown

when she died
she left
layaways
all over
the city

instead of canada

it was during the vietnam war
and jamie macdougal
was tall and skinny
wore his hair to his shoulders
with a fu manchu moustache
a belt fitted with pockets
for six different size harmonicas
which he played as he sang
why don't we do it in the road

when the draft board called
he came next door to borrow a dress
he picked the fitted iridescent green
with the nehru collar and tiny cloth
buttons all the way down the front
i don't know what color shoes he wore
but i bet they matched his harmonica belt

leaving a trail

clouds billow above the mountains
three or four spirals of gray
connect them to earth
everything is still
the hills so close
i could touch them
cows stand like toy statues
on the muted green
spreading across the flatness
black tree trunks line the road
their bare branches reaching upward

i am on my way to say goodbye again
leave a love note but it is too sad too silly
i turn my car around and head north

a fuzzy haired woman in a primed datsun z
is throwing bits of paper out the window
pieces of her life that glitter
and zigzag to the ground
leaving a trail

people ask me how I like living in petaluma

store owners dress up for halloween
you can have a conversation with tellers at the bank
brides register their gift wishes at tomasini hardware
the ragged palm trees in hill park blow in the afternoon breeze
the river and the railroad wind their way through town
hells angels suited business men and women
dancing down the street with brief cases chicken floats
highlights of the butter and eggs day parade
trees shade buckling sidewalks in front of old victorians
a & w carhops on roller skates deliver cherry cokes
shy smiles the exxon angel guards petaluma
her silver wings spread out over the city
the d street drawbridge lifts its weight to let boats pass
you can put your ear to the rail and hear its mournful cry
you can see donna all day every day pushing her shopping cart
all over town mark disuvero's sculptures reach up
towards blue sky connecting us to other worlds
the red sun disappears behind the silhouette of hills
the sky turning pink and peach and pale yellow
country is just a little way out of town

at the post office at 4th and d

a woman could feed dollar bills into the
stamp machine listen to the whining sound
as it accepts or rejects them
push in the numbers and hear
the dull thud as
the cardboard package hits the metal

unlock her post office box and look inside
past the open diamond shapes to the green desk
where the gray haired man sits beneath the sign
"paul's place"
stand at the glass topped table
with the tiger legs with claw feet
look up at the pale blue ceiling trimmed with gold

turn and look out the arched windows to the park
its dark limbed trees moving in the wind
homeless men huddled at a picnic table
drinking from a bottle in a bag
their burnt out faces sticking in her mind

she could get in her beat up cadillac
and drive out of town to the sweet smell
of wild mustard higher than the car
drive past the plowed and planted fields
cut and sectioned on the sloping hills

she could stop at the side of the road
and ask the man with the broken semi
if he needed help the smell
of diesel spilling in around her
and think of greasy hands
with black edged nails
slipping
inside her
she could moan

how ray spent last winter

ray is back
his hair and beard longer
he stands in front of the op center rolling a
cigarette
a cup of coffee at his feet

i ask him where he's been
down south because it's dryer
barstow because they have cheap motels
he had a tv and a bathroom he says
but no refrigerator
watched tv a lot
the olympics
and stars on ice
decided he wanted to see it in person

so he chased the show across the country
on a greyhound bus
all the way to south carolina
where he stayed in a shelter because
he spent his money getting there
but he got to see it

ray is smiling as he tells me
he's looking for a place
one with bare walls
so he can collage them

the red shoes

i slip on these red
sling back high heels
smooth my black stockings
just a minute
my legs are tan
no stockings
i pull on a short black skirt
no no
it's a long skirt
with a slit up the front
yes
right to the middle of my thigh
then my little red ruffled
no no no the blouse
is gray satin
tailored
open to the tops of the breasts
just enough to show
some black lace
add the antique jacket
i bought
at the peddler's fair in Benicia
pin my hair up
with a big red hibiscus
and head to the city
to perry's on union street
walk into the bar
sit down crossing
uncrossing my legs
smile and order a martini
dry and straight up
the bartender is attentive
everyone is looking
some will start a conversation
small talk
i'll smile chat
sip my martini

i can't have a cigarette
i stopped smoking
that's out
even in my fantasy
i'll sit for a while
then get up
walk out into the night alone
take off my red shoes
and drive barefoot
all the way home

ray gunn

at the homeless center
ray is looking for a quarter
for the dryer
i tell him i'll give him one
if he comes to the collage class
and he does

a week later i see him in line at the kitchen
he comes running over when he sees me
says he's got to tell me something

ever since he did the collage class
every where he looks he sees collage
in the street
the newspaper
magazines
on tv
he's collaging the walls in his room
he says

thirty years later

i can hold the room in my hand
the dull walls
the dark line of ants
coming up the metal night stand
to the bowl of pale green grapes
rows and rows of iron beds
filled with bleached white men
in non-descript gowns

and faces
my father runs his fingers
through his hair
what day is it
what year is it mr mifflin
the doctor asks
inside the bedstand drawer
a shaving brush
and razor

wrapped in tissue a gold-tone
elgin watch ticks off the hours
my husband is too nervous to shave him
so we bring in leonard the hair dresser
daddy smiled then looked confused
later they put him in a smaller room
crowded with long beds of dying men
outside in the hall a cadaver
sheet covered big toe tagged

daddy is getting whiter and whiter
with a yellow tinge
we drizzle water from a straw
into his desiccated mouth
the room stinks of urine
and pinesol
all night we sit

my sister nancy fingers a rosary
daddy a mormon is visited

by the laymen of the church
daddy is taking a long time to die
he doesn't know us
we stand in the hall
or by his bed
or at home by the phone

talking to the dead

mona
connie gave me your
little fuchsia hat
she wore it whenever
she went on a plane

i don't remember you
ever wearing it
sometimes i picture you
and mother
sitting at the kitchen table
smoking and drinking coffee

mother working on crossword puzzles
you doing your face
all the makeup paraphernalia
lined up in front of you
on the plastic table cloth

you trying on this color or that
for your eyes or cheeks or lips
always asking
how does this look
how about this one
driving us crazy
you did the same thing with clothes
going on and on for hours
i swear you tried on every
friggin thing in that wardrobe
mother and daddy gave you

and every time you put something on
you had to ask
how does this look what about this

and your hair my god that hair
long honey-colored blond
asking about this style or that

you drove us crazy
but you were the one
who had the breakdown

at san francisco general
you seemed more content less worried
of course you were medicated

the people you became friendly with
in there were nice
i liked the lady who worried about her son
getting killed on a plane
remember
she got out and a few months later
she and her family got killed in a plane crash
all except her son

goddam mona
you were driving me crazy a lot of the time
but you were fun
remember when we sat up all night at jacks bar
and talked through the night until morning
the swampers were mopping the floors when we left
it was the night before your cancer operation
but that's not what killed you
it was a stroke
it was because they put you in that recovery home
with all those old people dying

i think you gave up
connie believes it too
she says they killed you
my god mona
you were only 52

just before easter

i'm driving past the pope's church
you know
the big too pink job on 6th and bassett

and there's this stretch limo
parked at the front door
and there's this guy carrying a wooden cross
up the front steps and i think
maybe i should go inside
and pray or something
maybe light some candles
throw myself across the melting wax
the tiny glowing flames
tie my body to the mary statue
wrap myself up
in the tasseled cloth draped across
the altar table

and wait

stone angels

for john and tony

at the italian cemetery
stone angels
stand on mossy headstones
fingers pressed together
thick eyelids lowered
wings spread behind them

i find one not like the others
there is a movement
folds of garments floating out
into a dance
full wings fly up
from smooth round shoulders

it is the face
the chiseled smile
the open eyes
glistening
in the morning light

this is the one
i pick for you

all night diner

at three am
even the prostitutes
have left two
and three dollar tips

their grotesque angel faces
disappearing in the night
the bus-boys and the cook
are sleeping in the back

side work all done
salt pepper and sugars filled
ice melts in the bins
i'm the only one left out front

i sit in my soiled uniform
my apron weighted down with change
no one will be coming in till 5 or 6
i fight the urge to lie down

in a booth and sleep
and sit instead and read the menu
memorizing specials and the prices
i fix myself a cup of coffee

and some orange juice
it is so still my eyes play tricks
the toaster on the salad station
reflects images

spoons stretch out of shape
on the tables
the front door grows tall
there are no people going by outside

my fingers and my arms go numb
i get up and wipe the place down
for the hundredth time
i sit out the morning
counting tips

it's 90 plus

i'm driving down 101
to san mateo
to see tony's sister fil
a dirty haze hangs over the skyline
cars move in slow motion
a pickup hits a 7-up can
flips it up end over end
in the air

spewing yellow liquid
in a wide arch
the sun lighting each crystal

fil has leukemia
she looks pale and shrunken
when you're 80 anything can happen
she says
i feel sorry for the people
who come to see me
i get so tired i have to lie down
i can't even enjoy my death

her hair is sticking out
in every direction on her head
this is the first time i've seen her
not wearing one of her terrible wigs

she remembers the last time we had lunch
the fun we had

back on the freeway heading north
everything has stopped
i can hear every grinding moving
metal part of every passing car

read this:

It's not easy ~~being a fish in the nineties. But thanks to Honda's long-time commitment~~ to ~~clean water, at least they~~ have ~~one less thing~~ to think ~~about~~ these days.

Since ~~1973,~~ we've ~~manufactured and~~ sold ~~Only remarkably~~ clean and ~~surprisingly~~ quiet four-~~stroke outboard motors.~~

~~Unlike typical two-stroke marine engines, which deposit unburned fuel and oil in the water, Honda outboards feature recirculating oil systems. So the~~ oil ~~stays where it belongs: in the engine. Plus, our outboards are more fuel efficient and as much as ninety percent cleaner for hydrocarbon emissions.~~

~~All of which proves that~~ when it comes to the environment, ~~Honda is always thinking. with all of~~ our ~~products, from cars to power equipment, we work to balance~~ our desire ~~for fun and performance with society's need for clean air and clean water.~~

~~Something we're sure all our underwater friends appreciate when~~ attempting to decide which minnows are really minnows.

walking the dog

when hot dogger dewey weber
master of the power turn
died
he was fifty-three and still riding

dewey wasn't great on big waves
he was great on two-foot curls
running to the nose
hanging ten
staying there longer

he could turn a fifty-cent wave
into a five-dollar ride
tuck himself into the hottest corner
the box seat where the wave peaks up
and starts breaking
drops straight down the slope
made his famous power turn
at the bottom and beat the wave

dewey said
"you have to unweight your body"

a dancer would understand that

heels

at lenora's vintage resale shop i come across
a young boy of ten or eleven trying on high heels

i tell him try on the tan sling backs and he does
his mother yelling from the next room where she's

looking at dresses with his little sister
"stop trying on those high heels franklin"

we stand there together picking through the shelves
of not quite worn out pairs

his mom sticks her head in the door
and tells him he's tried on enough for now

"i just wonder how they feel how you can walk in them"
he says pulling on black t-straps with french heels

the kind that make you wobble
he gets up and teeters toward the mirror

"look at these aren't they cool"
his mother's reflection right behind him

robert mitchum

i am fourteen
standing outside
the golden gate theater
waiting for robert mitchum
to come out so i can get
his autograph and he does
dressed in a dark gray overcoat
he smiles the same smile
that stretches across the screen
i stand there shivering
in my thin cotton dress
he offers his coat

it's not a dream
i'm standing there in the
dark dampness of the evening
a bright light streaming
from the doorway
i can't speak

it starts to rain i can feel
light drops catching my hair

he's talking about his wife
just having a baby
someone asks him about the trouble
the marijuana bust
he smiles tips his hat
shoves his hands deep into his pockets
and walks down the alley
to a limo standing at the curb

the noe show

i'm working as an usherette
in my burgundy uniform with gold stripes
frankenstein and the three stooges is playing
and nobody i mean nobody
not even the kids from my school
in their scuffed white suedes
and turned up levis
will get into the loges without a ticket

it's my job i tell myself
the frankenstein monster growls and lunges
the three stooges trip over one another
with frankenstein stumbling after them
his crooked smile and soulful eyes
stretching across the screen
as a young girl in the balcony screams out

FRANKIE! you're breaking my heart

blue sky

"right now my whole life is magic"
                                    —al young

blue sky a cloud you kissing
her throat a soft kiss then dipping
her body back the two of you
hanging together in mid air
the little dog

yelping

going red

he knew that riding west into the sun
could make him blind
he rode up the small town street
caught a glimpse of red lips
made a too sharp turn to go back
his front wheel hit the curb
bounced up into the air
setting him free
to sail through the warm afternoon
his body leaving the cushioned seat
his feet lifting off the metal pegs
watching the black and chrome of his
riderless machine coasting along the walk
red lips   red sun   red sky
he was above it all
soaring through the stillness
toward his reflection
in the plate glass window
his body gliding toward
it's mirrored image
a frozen moment
just before the jagged splinters
cut into his leather pants
tore through the dark blue shirt
one long shard stuck in his throat
so that every time he took a breath
the red ran down the sidewalk
he lay there looking up
red moon red sky

i believe

in myself
light rain
sudden storms
the moon
polenta and sausage
good sex
red sunsets
a perfect martini
the stars
true love
monet's garden
cracked crab
long baths
soft jazz
a walk on the beach
and root beer floats

i believe
in quiet mornings
the ocean
slow dancing
the back of a man's neck
fred astair tapping across the screen
the magic of the sacramento delta
stone angels in italian cemeteries
growing your own tomatoes
paul newman's eyes
that writing poetry is telling the truth
doing crafts is in my blood
ironing is therapy
kissing is an art
and dusting is a waste of time